SIGMUND FREUD

Doctor of the Mind

Marilyn Lager

Drawings by Eric Lager

ENSLOW PUBLISHERS, INC.

Bloy St. & Ramsey Ave.   P.O. Box 38
Box 777   Aldershot
Hillside, N.J. 07205   Hants GU12 6BP
U.S.A.   U.K.

This book is dedicated to Karen, Jennifer, and Robert

The author would like to thank her husband, Eric Lager, M.D., for his knowledge, technical assistance, and drawings used in the book.

Certain quotations on pages 10, 14, 21, 25, and 28 are from *An Autobiographical Study* by Sigmund Freud, translated by James Strachey, and are used with permission of W.W. Norton & Company, Inc. Copyright renewed 1963 by James Strachey.

Certain quotations on pages 12 and 34 are from *The Interpretation of Dreams* by Sigmund Freud, translated and edited by James Strachey. Published in the U.S. by Basic Books, Inc. by arrangement with George Allen and Unwin Ltd. and The Hogarth Press, Ltd. Reprinted by permission of the publishers.

Letters on pages 19, 20, and 52 are from *Letters of Sigmund Freud*, selected and edited by Ernst L. Freud, translated by Tania & James Stern. © 1960 by Sigmund Freud Copyrights Ltd. Reprinted by permission of Basic Books, Inc., Publishers.

Certain quotations on pages 13, 14, 46, 51, and 56 are from *The Life and Work of Sigmund Freud*, Volumes I, II, and III, by Ernest Jones. © 1953, 1955, and 1957 by Ernest Jones. Reprinted by permission of Basic Books, Inc., Publishers.

Cover photograph courtesy of National Library of Medicine.

Library of Congress Cataloging in Publication Data

Lager, Marilyn
    Sigmund Freud, doctor of the mind.

    Bibliography: p.
    Includes index.
    Summary: A brief biography of the Austrian doctor who spent his life analyzing the mind and its illnesses.
    1. Freud, Sigmund, 1856-1939—Juvenile literature. 2. Psychoanalysts—Austria—Biography—Juvenile literature. [1. Freud, Sigmund, 1856-1939. 2. Psychiatrists] I. Title.
BF173.F85L24   1986   150.19'52 [B] [92]   85-20416
ISBN 0-89490-117-6

Printed in the United States of America

10 9 8 7 6 5 4 3 2 1

Contents

FOREWORD

The heroes and heroines of our society are most often those people who have had an important effect on our understanding of the world or on the way we live our lives. They have made contributions in a wide variety of fields, including the arts, sciences, literature, sports, and the humanities. They come from all races, cultures, and geographic areas, and they share in common a dedication to advancing our civilization in some way.

Sigmund Freud was one of these heroes. He was an inventive, creative, and courageous physician who was born in Europe in the latter part of the nineteenth century. He was able to weave the threads of the observations and insights which he noticed as he listened to his patients into an organized and logical theory of human psychology. This theory formed the basis of much of our current understanding of psychological development and is the foundation of modern psychoanalysis.

In this book, you will find the story of his life and his work, and you will learn how events and experiences influence us, as they influenced Freud. His genius lay in the way he could learn from both the ordinary and unusual events of his life and his time, understanding the mysteries of the mind, to formulate and develop his unique contributions.

Carol C. Nadelson, M.D.

Associate Psychiatrist-In-Chief and
Director, Training and Education
    Department of Psychiatry
    New England Medical Center, Inc.
Professor and Vice-Chairman
    Department of Psychiatry
    Tufts University
President
    American Psychiatric Association

Introduction

Sigmund Freud was a medical doctor. But he did not use a stethoscope, give injections, or perform surgery. Freud was not a doctor of the body. He was a doctor of the mind.

It is important to understand the difference between the mind and the brain. Of course, the brain is part of the body. We need our brain to think and feel. But *what* we think and feel is expressed by the idea of mind. There can be no mind without the brain, but to study the mind requires different methods from those used to examine the brain.

The mind affects how we behave. When a person behaves in a strange or unusual way, it may be that his mind is impaired or it may be that his brain is impaired. For example, a person may forget how a car accident happened because his brain was injured in the accident. But he may have forgotten the accident because he was afraid to remember it. In that case, we would say that the disturbance is in the mind. The treatment for each

1

cause of forgetting is different. In long, severe mental illness, however, doctors cannot always separate mental from physical impairment. Treatment is usually aimed at both the mind and the brain. Whatever the cause of the problem, its treatment is medical.

This was not always so. Centuries ago, the mind was considered part of a person's spiritual or religious experience that must be treated by priests or spiritual healers. People with disturbances of the mind were seen as possessed by evil spirits or demons. So the priests or healers tried to get rid of the demons. This often caused agony to the disturbed person. Holes might be drilled in the sick person's skull to let the demons escape. The "healers" might try to drive the "devils" out. They would torture the person by burning, flogging, or starving. Certain women who behaved in strange ways were thought to be witches and were burned at the stake. Some of these people may have had disturbances of the mind. Some may have had impaired brains. Others may simply have had ideas that made those in power uneasy.

Compassion for mentally disturbed people grew slowly. Institutions kept the insane away from the normal. But in these places, the mentally ill were mixed in with criminals and were treated cruelly. They were chained in cold and filthy cells infested with rats. Often they were left naked with only a ragged blanket to cover them. At a large hospital in England, called Bedlam, the mentally disturbed were exhibited, as if at a circus. For a penny, one could watch the insane rant and rave, tear at themselves, or make strange gestures and noises.

A great day for the mentally ill came in 1795. Philippe Pinel, a doctor at a mental institution in France, cut the chains of the inmates. Some of them had not seen the sun or walked for forty years. He realized that for many of these patients, the illness was in the mind. He suspected that the treatment would be mental, rather than physical. This meant rest and trying to persuade them to act normally.

Still, there was great uncertainty about how to treat the mentally ill. An American physician, Benjamin Rush, pointed out the importance of kindness toward the mental patient. But even he invented a chair in which the patient was to be whirled about for hours! Kind words would help, he wrote, but so would icy showers and bloodletting. Or the unfortunate patient might have to endure complete darkness or be packed in camphor. If patients got well, it was in spite of such treatments, not because of them.

By the eighteenth century, physicians were turning to new discoveries in science. One such physician, Anton Mesmer, believed that there was a magnetic flow through the body and that disturbances in this flow caused mental illness. He placed magnets on the body in an attempt to change the magnetic forces. He stroked the patient at the same time. In 1774, a patient suffering from fainting spells, vomiting, and pain came to Mesmer. There seemed to be no physical cause for her suffering. Such patients were called hysterics. Today we know that their symptoms result from disturbances of the mind. After repeated treatment by Mesmer's method, she was cured. Later, Mesmer decided that it was not the magnets at all that had cured the patient. Rather, he thought that the stroking had relaxed her. He believed, though, that stroking channeled a force called "animal magnetism." Animal magnetism became very popular in Europe and America. It was often practiced by people who simply wanted to make money. But it did lead to a very important discovery: the discovery of hypnosis.

Hypnosis is a state resembling sleep. A hypnotist can command a person to perform acts never possible in waking life. This showed doctors a curious thing. They saw that some mentally ill patients, such as hysterics, could give up symptoms and behave normally, at least temporarily, under hypnosis. A well person, on the other hand, could be commanded to take on symptoms of such an illness.

The discovery and use of hypnosis influenced scientists in the nineteenth century to distinguish between what was physical and what was mental. This was no easy task. Even the great French physician Jean Martin Charcot, who used hypnosis in the study of hysteria, believed that the cause of that illness was damage to the brain.

Toward the end of the nineteenth century, Sigmund Freud, a student of Charcot, began to practice neurology in Vienna. He also began as a hypnotist who stroked his hysterical patients on the head. In this way, his treatment was like all previous "treatments" of the mentally ill. In all those treatments, something was done to patients, whether it was drilling holes in their skulls, whirling them in chairs, or persuading or hypnotizing them. When Freud gave up hypnosis, he turned from doing something to a patient to helping the patient do something for himself. By insisting that the patient reveal everything on his mind, he helped him understand his deepest thoughts and feelings. Freud developed this "talking treatment" into psychoanalysis. Even though today medications are of great benefit in the treatment of mental illness, Sigmund Freud's discoveries remain extremely important in understanding the mind.

1

The Big, Black Train

Three-year-old Sigmund sat on the front step of his house. The small town of Freiberg was awakening. Inside the house, his mother and father, already wide awake, prepared for a journey. They were dressing his baby sister Anna. His mother called out, "Hurry, dear Sigi, we must be ready when our horse and carriage arrives."

From the tall steeple that loomed over the town, Sigmund heard the church bells chime. He covered his ears. He heard his mother call again, "Hurry, Sigmund, we must not miss our train. We must be ready." Young Sigmund wasn't ready. He did not want to leave his friends or his house, where Mr. Zajic, the locksmith, had his shop. But now a horse and carriage approached the door.

Sigmund's father came out of the house, took his hand, and then lifted him aboard the carriage. He tucked him safely into the seat, and the little boy turned to look at the house. But where was Sigmund's mother? Wasn't she going away too? The horse began to move restlessly. The little boy was suddenly afraid.

Yes, there she was, moving quickly out of the door, holding baby Anna, and entering the carriage. Now the horse trotted swiftly, and Sigmund's house began to move away. The Freud family was going on a journey, a journey to a new home, a new life, and, for Sigmund, a new world.

Sigmund didn't know where they were going or why they were leaving. He knew that he loved the beautiful soft green fields they were passing and the deep, dark forests of tall fir trees where his father had often walked with him. Could he be leaving these?

They lived above the locksmith's house.

Soon they reached the train station. Sigmund caught sight of the big, black train, which belched out thick smoke and hissed menacingly. His mother held Anna tightly as she climbed up the steps. His father swung him aboard. The train started slowly. Then it carried them harshly and joltingly through the day and into the night.

Sigmund slept poorly and cried out often. Once, through the window, he glimpsed the night sky, lit by the burning fires of industrial gas jets. The smoke and the loud noise of the brakes frightened him. He lay back exhausted in his mother's arms.

Sigmund was too young to understand why his family was leaving Freiberg. His father, Jakob Freud, was having business problems. He was a wool merchant, and he was Jewish. Times were hard in 1859 for many businessmen. And in Eastern Europe, Jews were often blamed for whatever difficulties happened. That was how it was in the provincial town of Freiberg, Moravia. The natives turned against the Jewish merchants. In the cities to the west, people were more enlightened. A merchant and his wool could be judged for their own qualities and not for the religion of the merchant. Jakob would try his luck in Leipzig, Germany.

But if the train could carry Sigmund away from his home, couldn't it also carry him away from his parents? Even though they were with him, he was afraid that they would be left behind, just as the forests and the bright clear skies speeding by the windows of the train were left behind.

The three-year-old Sigmund could not understand what was happening. But years later, when he grew to be a man, this experience of leaving his home and his fear of losing his parents still stayed alive in his mind. His fear of trains continued. He would come to understand that many adults who suffered from unreasonable fears were afraid because something fearful had happened to them when they were small children. He would remember his childhood. In making the connection between the fears of adults and their childhood experiences, he would discover a new science of the mind.

Sigmund caught sight of
the big, black train.

2

"Golden Sigi"

Sigmund's parents didn't leave him as he feared they would. After a year in Leipzig, Jakob, dissatisfied with business conditions there, moved the family again. This time they went to Vienna, the capital city of Austria. Vienna was a fine city with beautiful green parks, ornate palaces, great stone statues of men on horseback, glistening fountains, and elegant shops. But Sigmund missed the country. Still, Jakob had time for young Sigmund. They took walks through the city, went ice skating, and had good long talks.

Most important, Jakob had time to teach Sigmund to read and write and to love books and learning. Jakob was Sigmund's main teacher until he was nine years old. Sigmund enjoyed his lessons. He was proud and happy to show how much he knew. Learning came easily to him.

As Sigmund grew up, he felt he had a special responsibility to be strong and smart. He was the first child of his young mother, Amalie, and he was clever from his earliest years. He knew his mother loved him. How lucky he was that even though his mother had six more children, she seemed to favor him for the rest of her life. She called him "my golden Sigi."

Sigmund had been born in a caul, which is a thin extra layer of skin, usually around the skull of an infant. A caul was unusual and was thought to be lucky. "Am I lucky because of that caul," thought Sigmund later, "or am I able to be happy and successful because my mother *wants* me to be?" He certainly delighted his mother.

His sisters, Anna, Rosa, and Marie, who were only a few years younger than he, became his pupils. He gave them tests and made sure he approved of the books they read. They all respected him and his love for learning. Only Sigmund had an oil lamp in his bedroom. His parents and sisters had to read by candlelight!

One day, Sigmund came out of his room with a frown on his face. Anna was being coached on the piano by her mother. Sigmund complained, "I can't study. The piano disturbs me." So the Freuds got rid of the piano! Sigmund's studies were so important to the family that they did whatever they could to help him. After all, hadn't an old woman told Amalie at Sigmund's birth that she had brought a great man into the world?

"I must have taught you well," said Jakob one morning. "You have passed your examination to attend Sperlgymnasium." Sigmund, at nine years old, entered Sperl, a combined junior and senior high school in Vienna. Although he was one of the youngest students to enter, he wrote later: "I was at the top of my class for seven years; I enjoyed special privileges there, and had scarcely ever to be examined in class."

Reading engrossed and absorbed him. In fact, his great love for books and learning once led to a disagreement with his father when Sigmund bought more books than he could afford. He learned enough Spanish, Italian, English, Latin, and Greek to

They had time for long walks through Vienna.

read books in those languages. When he was only eight years old, he developed a taste for Shakespeare's plays. At home, he was most often found reading in his "cabinet." This small, narrow room, which was also his bedroom, overflowed with books on every subject. Conversation on every subject flowed, too, when he invited friends into his cabinet to talk.

Sigmund loved to read about wars and heroes. Alexander the Great, a Macedonian general and king, was a favorite. Sigmund wished to be a brave conqueror, as Alexander was.

When Sigmund was ten, his mother gave birth to a baby boy. Sigmund and his sisters were asked to suggest a name for the baby. Anna, Rosa, Marie, Dolfi, and even little Paula had proposals ready.

"Julius," Anna sang out, "to name him after our baby brother who died."

"Otto," shouted Rosa, "so he can read his name backwards!"

"I would like him to be called Alexander," said Sigmund, "for Alexander the Great was the first conqueror of the world!" Alexander it was.

Sigmund admired bravery. When Jakob told him of how a man had knocked off his new fur cap, hurling it into the mud, Sigmund was shocked. The man had shouted, "Jew, get off the pavement!" Sigmund asked Jakob what he had done, and Jakob replied, "I went into the roadway and picked up my cap." This made Sigmund angry and ashamed. Was his father a coward? Why had he not fought back?

Perhaps Jakob knew how difficult it was for Jews to fight back at that time in Europe, but his young son was shaken. He felt that people must fight for what is right. Sigmund himself would have to have the courage to stand by his ideas when others mocked them. Like Alexander the Great, he would become a courageous conqueror.

3

The Young Doctor

Sigmund graduated from Sperl with highest honors. He was seventeen. Jakob's pride in his bright son was enormous. He knew how Sigmund had loved the English language and its literature almost since he had first learned to read. He rewarded Sigmund for his outstanding performance at Sperl with a trip to England. Sigmund looked forward to this trip for two years, journeying to England when he was nineteen.

When Sigmund returned, a sense of pleasure with the English remained with him. He was impressed that Jews were treated with more respect there than in Austria. He observed, with appreciation, a "sensitive feeling for justice of its inhabitants," which he wrote about later. His wish to live in England had been born. It was to remain with him all his life.

After graduation, Sigmund was unsure about what he should do next in his life. It seemed that in Vienna a Jew would choose a career only in medicine, law, or business. Sigmund's father urged him to decide for himself.

Sigmund decided to be a doctor. His decision was not based so much on a desire to relieve the suffering of individual patients as it was on an interest in studying the nature of life. "I was moved, rather, by a sort of curiosity, which was, however, directed more towards human concerns than towards natural objects . . ." he was to write later. Medical studies would provide the best means to achieve this goal. He entered the University of Vienna as a medical student in 1873.

In his fourth year of medical school, Sigmund began working in the physiology laboratory of Dr. Ernst Brücke. Physiology is the study of how living things and their parts work. It was physiology that really interested Sigmund, and it was Dr. Brücke, a physiology professor, who inspired him and became his model of a man of science. Brücke respected and sought original ideas. He was exacting in his demand for truth, regardless of the consequences. "He is the greatest authority I ever met," said Sigmund. Dr. Brücke's flashing eyes and quick temper delighted him. He admired this much older man as a young son might admire his father.

Dr. Brücke assigned Sigmund the study of nerve cells of lower animals. Lower animals, such as worms, are less complicated and usually smaller than higher animals, such as apes or humans. One morning, Sigmund called excitedly to Dr. Brücke, "Herr Doctor, you must come. I have something of interest to show you." Sigmund showed under the microscope that the nerve cells of higher and lower animals were constructed in similar ways and of similar matter. "Dr. Brücke," Sigmund exclaimed, "don't you think that nerve cells in the human brain must work in the same way as nerve cells in the brain of a fish?" "This is

He studied nerve cells under a microscope.

an important scientific discovery for a young man to make," Brücke encouraged Sigmund. "You must publish this." Sigmund published these findings when he was twenty-one years old.

Sigmund later found that he could see the nerve cells better under the microscope if he stained them with gold chloride. This unique method helped him gain new knowledge about nerve cell pathways. He knew that to uncover new facts one often had to discover a new way to see them.

At about this time, Sigmund was drafted into the Austrian army. As a medical student he stood around in the army hospital and was bored most of the time. His boyhood wish to plan attacks and fight heroic battles was not stirred in the army. No longer did he want to become a great general—or even a soldier. Now he had other conquests in mind.

Sigmund returned to medical school and passed his final examinations. In March 1881, Sigmund Freud became a certified doctor. He stayed on in Dr. Brücke's laboratory.

One day, Dr. Brücke looked over Sigmund's shoulder as he sat bent over his microscope. The professor expressed concern that here in this laboratory, Sigmund could not advance himself and would find neither money nor position. Surely Sigmund's father could not continue to support his grown son. He was not rich. If Sigmund were to become a doctor in his own practice, he might earn a comfortable living.

So Sigmund reluctantly gave up his beloved Professor Brücke and his careful research. He found work with patients in the clinics of the General Hospital of Vienna. His interest in treating medical illness or in doing surgery was not great, and he felt that he had lost his direction in science.

Then he transferred to the Neuropsychiatry Clinic, and his excitement about how things worked in nature was sparked again. Here he learned from Dr. Theodor Meynert, a brain anatomist, about the workings of the human brain. He learned how damage to the brain could cause people to become permanently paralyzed, losing the ability to move their arms and legs. Here he saw other patients who were also paralyzed but who seemed to recover, only to get worse again. He wondered if the cause of their trouble was something other than damage to the brain, as was then commonly thought. There was no cure for brain damage. But if such illnesses were not caused by damaged brain cells, perhaps a cure could be found. Here was a new direction, a possibility for new discoveries.

4

"My Dear Sweet Girl"

One evening after work, Sigmund entered his family's apartment, ready to continue his studies in his cabinet, as he did every night. But on this occasion, he was struck by the gay laughter and pleasant appearance of a visitor to his sisters, a young woman who sat in the parlor, casually enjoying an apple. He lingered by the door.

"Who is this girl?" he asked as he pulled Marie aside.

"Ah, this is Martha Bernays, Sigmund, and she is a dear person. Come, you must meet her."

Sigmund joined the group. There were no studies for him that night, for he was immediately drawn to Martha's gentle yet merry nature. Very soon they became better acquainted. They took long strolls through the parks of Vienna, and he began to send her a rose every day. From this early time, he called her "Princess."

Only a few months later, Martha and Sigmund became secretly engaged. They could not announce a definite time to be married because they could not afford to live together on their own. The situation worsened when Martha told him one day that she had bad news—her mother had decided to move her family out of Vienna to Germany.

For Martha and Sigmund, this was the beginning of four years of separations and longing, of visits and partings—and letters, 900 of them in all!

Martha and Sigmund wrote to each other often.

In many of the letters he expressed his frustrations about not having enough money to get married.

> "Oh, my darling Marty, how poor we are! Suppose we were to tell the world we are planning to share life and they were to ask us: What is your dowry?—Nothing but our love for each other."

He was not content simply to declare his love for Martha, but he probed the nature of it. The following letter gave an early indication of his love and his interest in the workings of the mind. He showed how love can be painful too.

> "Why don't we fall in love with a different person every month? Because at each separation a part of our heart would be torn away. Why don't we make a friend of everyone? Because the loss of him or any misfortune befalling him would affect us deeply."

In a letter from his travels to Germany in 1883, he wrote Martha with pride about how he didn't back down when an angry mob turned on him in a train in an argument that began with a difference about an open window.

> ". . . there came a shout from the background: "He's a dirty Jew!"—And with this the whole situation took on a different color . . . . Even a year ago I would have been speechless with agitation, but now I am different; I was not in the least frightened of that mob, asked the one to keep to himself his empty phrases which inspired no respect in me, and the other to step up and take what was coming to him."

Perhaps he was trying to undo the humiliation which his father accepted when he picked his hat up out of the gutter long ago. Some sons are so disappointed by their father's lack of courage that they go to great lengths, sometimes even to reck-lessness, to prove their own. Freud may have been such a son.

Whatever the reasons for his boldness, he seemed to have a clear picture of how, at age twenty-eight, he intended his life to be. He knew it would not be an ordinary one. In this letter to Martha, he writes to his "beloved treasure,"

> "I am very stubborn and very reckless and need great challenges; I have done a number of things which any sensible person would be bound to consider very rash. For example, to take up science as a poverty-stricken man, then as a poverty-stricken man to capture a poor girl—but this must continue to be my way of life: risking a lot, hoping a lot, working a lot."

That Sigmund was willing to risk a lot was evident in his hope for the drug cocaine, which he regarded almost as a cure-all. He wrote Martha:

> "I am also toying now with a project and a hope which I will tell you about; . . . It is a therapeutic experiment . . . . cocaine, . . . I am certainly going to try it . . ."

He took the drug himself and prescribed it for others too freely without considering its harmful and addictive effects.

On the other hand, cocaine was to prove to be an invaluable anesthetic for surgery on the surface of the body such as the skin or the eye. Freud had suggested this to a friend, Carl Koller, an eye doctor who made experiments and presented the results to the medical world. Freud rushed to finish his own scientific paper on cocaine, without including the mention of this use, in order to travel to Germany to be with Martha. So he missed the opportunity to describe what turned out to be the only legitimate use of cocaine—that of a local anesthetic.

Freud wrote later, ". . . how it was the fault of my fiancée that I was not already famous at that youthful age . . . . Koller is therefore rightly regarded as the discoverer of local anaesthesia by cocaine, which has become so important in minor surgery; but I bore my fiancée no grudge for the interruption."

But cocaine had only been a side interest. What had excited him most were the workings of the mind that could be studied through mental illness. He became particularly interested in a condition called hysteria, from which patients could recover. But there was little to be learned about this from doctors in Vienna. So he determined to go to Paris to see what he could learn from the leading authority on the subject. From Paris, letters to his "dear sweet girl" continued to flow, filled with enthusiasm for what he was learning and hopes, most of all, for their marriage.

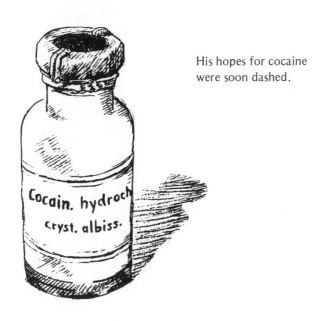

His hopes for cocaine were soon dashed.

5

The Mind Influences the Body

Freud competed for and won a small grant of money to study neurology in Paris with a renowned neurologist, Dr. Jean Martin Charcot. Neurology is the treatment of disorders of the brain and nervous system. Freud knew that Charcot, the greatest neurologist of his time, was treating patients called hysterics by hypnotizing them. The serious attention Charcot paid to these patients and the brilliant demonstrations he gave made an enormous impression on Freud when he arrived in Paris.

Freud was encouraged that an authority such as Charcot was studying hysterics when other doctors did not consider them worthy of medical attention. Hysterics were patients who might act wildly or uncontrollably, shout or lose speech, or be unable to move their arms or legs. Even though they improved temporarily with hypnosis, Charcot believed that such patients had something physically wrong with their brains. He thought the damage had been caused by sudden injury to the nervous system.

Charcot, demonstrating a case of hysteria. (Lithograph, after the painting by Andre Brouillet.) *Courtesy, National Library of Medicine.*

Working with Charcot, Freud saw that a doctor could hypnotize a normal person. The doctor could influence the person to be unable to move an arm or leg, for instance, even when the person tried hard to do so. During the hypnotic trance, the hypnotist could command the subject to do something after he comes out of his trance and to forget the command. After the person does the act, he will not know why he did what he did. He then makes up a reason for his action because he has no memory of the command. He is totally unaware of the real reason for his action, which is that he is obeying the hypnotist's command.

Perhaps, reasoned Freud, hysterics are similar to normal people who are hypnotized. Perhaps they are also influenced by ideas of which they are not aware, but ideas of their own, not a hypnotist's. Maybe these ideas could cause them to be unable to move an arm or leg, just as the hypnotist's suggestions to his normal subjects could cause them to be unable to move an arm or leg. Maybe nothing is wrong with a hysteric's brain.

Freud returned to Vienna and began working as a neurologist. His curiosity about hysteria continued. Few patients came. Sigmund and Martha had no hope of marrying until they had the money to set up a proper home. In the summer of 1886, there was good news at last. Martha telegraphed Sigmund that an aunt had given the couple a generous gift of money. Soon an uncle gave more, and the marriage could take place.

So, on a beautiful day in September, Martha Bernays and Sigmund Freud stood together in the Town Hall of Wandsbek, Germany, and became husband and wife. Sigmund was a handsome, tanned thirty-year-old man with a fine dark beard and even features. Martha, at twenty-five, was slender and graceful. Their marriage was to last fifty-three years.

The couple lived in a four-room apartment in Vienna. Martha began decorating it immediately. Freud worried that he could not support Martha. He also had the responsibility of helping to support his parents and his sisters, who were still living at home.

Luckily, a respected and established physician, Dr. Josef Breuer, recognized Freud's abilities. Dr. Breuer sent patients to Freud and lent him money to pay for living expenses. "He became," Freud said, "my friend and helper in my difficult circumstances."

One day, a mother brought her fifteen-year-old daughter to him. The mother told him that her daughter had been diagnosed by several prominent neurologists in Vienna as having epilepsy.

Epilepsy is a disease of the brain, in which the patient suddenly loses consciousness and falls to the ground. In its more severe types, the limbs contract and finally flail out. The face turns blue, the mouth salivates, and the person may bite his tongue.

"I am especially frightened because of what happened during her last attack," the mother said. "We were on a camping trip in the mountains. Her father had made a small fire, and we were about to go to sleep when her attack began. During the attack, she was about to fall into the fire when she caught herself. Fortunately, she stumbled away before she fell. What if she had fallen into the fire?"

"She caught herself?" Freud asked.

"Yes," she said, "and stumbled away."

"Good," said Freud. "I think I can help you. Let me examine her."

He took the young patient to the examining room, where

he found no neurological disorder. Then he hypnotized the patient. He told her not to have another attack before he saw her again in a month. Then he brought her out of the trance.

Back in the consultation room, he assured the mother that her daughter would not have another attack and asked her to bring her back in a month. The mother, taking her daughter by the arm, left puzzled.

They returned gratefully a month later. The mother confirmed that her daughter had no recurrence of her attacks.

"It's like a miracle," she said. "How did you do it?"

"You told me that when she almost fell into the fire, she caught herself and stumbled away. A person with epilepsy has lost consciousness before he falls. If he were about to fall into a fire, he could not save himself. Hysterical attacks look very much like epilepsy, but the person does not really lose consciousness and will always manage to keep from harm when he falls. I diagnosed her as a hysteric and hypnotized her to keep her from having another attack," Freud explained.

"You mean she is cured!" exclaimed the mother.

"Not exactly. Cure by hypnosis does not last forever," Freud said, shaking his head. And in 1888, he wrote an article on hysteria in which he made note of the difference between hysteria and epilepsy.

Josef Breuer shared Freud's interest in hysterical patients. He had told Freud about a case that troubled him. The patient's name was Bertha Pappenheim. Freud had listened with great interest and had often thought about this case. He mused that there was something unique, something that might open a door to the understanding of mental illness in this case of Bertha Pappenheim.

6

The Talking Treatment

Bertha Pappenheim was a young woman whom Josef Breuer had been treating for some years. She complained of a paralyzed arm and neck. She had a strange nervous cough, had trouble speaking, and constantly squinted. She was diagnosed as a hysteric. Dr. Breuer had found that by hypnotizing her, he could help her remember the circumstances that led to the development of each of her symptoms.

She particularly remembered her feelings when her father had been sick before he died. How sad she had been! She had held back her tears so that she wouldn't disturb him when she sat by his bedside. Breuer helped her see that the strange squint she had now was like her squint in holding back her tears when she had been with her father. Her squint went away after she remembered this. So did her other symptoms as she remembered how they had first occurred. She called this the "talking cure" or "chimney sweeping," by which she meant that her mind had been cleared of painful memories by talking about them.

27

Now a curious thing became clear. Although she was better, Bertha could not stay well without Dr. Breuer. She felt that she loved him and could not think for herself or be independent of him. Dr. Breuer was disturbed and embarrassed by this, and he gave up her treatment. Then all her symptoms returned.

Freud had been very interested in Breuer's story. The case showed clearly how these strange symptoms of hysterics were a way of expressing ideas and emotions that could not be put into words because they were so painful.

"Josef," said Freud, "the case of Bertha should go first in a book about hysteria."

But Breuer was embarrassed about Bertha's "love" for him. He felt that perhaps he unknowingly had done something to encourage this young girl. Upset about the case, Breuer had left Vienna with his wife for an extended trip.

Freud eventually explained this "falling in love" of hysterical patients with their doctors. He told Breuer that a young patient had also flung her arms around his neck, but this didn't mean she really loved him or that he had done something improper. It was a symptom, Freud said, a sign of hysteria, which replaces the other symptoms. He was able to convince Breuer that they should write about this case and this treatment ". . . an invaluable discovery . . . making science the richer by it."

He continued to hypnotize patients, but some patients could not be hypnotized. He tried other methods, having patients lie on the couch, as with hypnosis. He urged them to recall how their symptoms began. Sometimes he would stroke their heads to help them, and he saw that they could remember even without hypnosis.

In his eagerness to understand, Freud prodded his patients about the beginning of their symptoms. He could not yet see the larger picture that would allow him to answer the questions not only about hysteria but about how the human mind works in general. Fortunately, he could let himself be helped by a patient, Elisabeth von R. Once, while prodding her to talk, she exclaimed that he should stop putting ideas into her head and listen to her! He did.

In 1895, Breuer and Freud published a book about hysteria. The case of Bertha Pappenheim was the first one described in the book. She was called Anna O. to protect her privacy. The last case, her name also changed, was the case of Elisabeth von R. But the world was not interested in the book. Breuer returned to his more standard medical practice, but Freud went on to solve the puzzle of hysteria.

There was something about the use of hypnosis that disturbed him. At first, he was not sure what it was. What gave the hypnotist such power over his subject? Was Charcot right that only hysterics could be hypnotized? Was this yet another symptom of hysteria? Was there a connection between the patient allowing himself to be hypnotized and "falling in love" with the doctor? Why did the "talking cure" not last?

Elisabeth von R. had helped him discover a new tool to replace hypnosis. He later called it "free association," meaning that the patient could say whatever came to mind without the doctor's interference. Freud used this tool in the same scientific way he had learned to use the microscope in Dr. Brücke's laboratory. This time what was before him for study was whatever came to the patient's mind, without concern for the politeness of ordinary conversation and without the doctor's control as during hypnosis.

He began to instruct patients at the beginning of treatment to try not to hold anything back. He saw them daily. He found that they would express love and hate for him. He felt strong enough himself not to have to react to their praise or blame. He encouraged them to say what they had feared to think.

Now the pieces of the puzzle of hysteria and hypnosis began to fit together. Lying on the couch, unable to see him because he sat behind them, with permission to say everything, the patients felt love, hate, and fear toward Freud. But these were not feelings for him as a real person but as they imagined him. Was this not what Bertha Pappenheim had experienced toward Dr. Breuer?

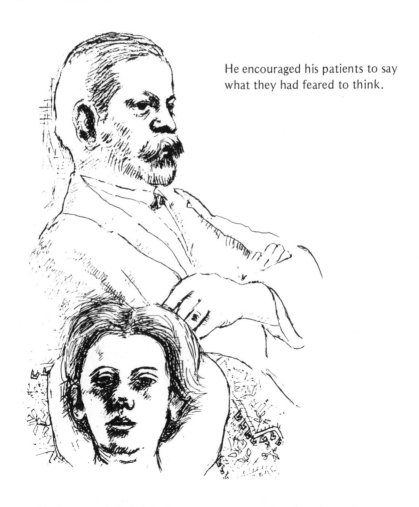

He encouraged his patients to say what they had feared to think.

The power of hypnosis now also yielded to explanation. In the hypnotic state, the patient imagines the hypnotist to be powerful. Under his instruction to do what he might otherwise be afraid to do, the patient gains strength and protection.

Hypnosis is an example of the power of love, but such love is not based in reality. In the long run, Freud knew, it weakened the hysterical patient more.

"I was right to distrust hypnosis," he thought. "By hypnotizing a patient we play into his belief that the strength is in the doctor and not in himself, so when the doctor leaves he feels helpless. When I let the patient speak freely, he may have the same belief, but because he is not in a trance, we can examine his feelings, study his mind by looking at everything in it, what is forbidden, what is unrealistic, even fantastic. It's an analysis of the mind—yes, a psychoanalysis, and this is what ultimately cures the patient."

This was in 1896, fourteen years after he first heard of the case of Bertha Pappenheim. Now Freud saw that because she had not been able to tolerate the death of her father, she had substituted Dr. Breuer in his place. She had behaved as if he were her father, as if her father had never died. Psychoanalysis led Freud to a conclusion he could not escape. This way of reacting had begun when Bertha was a small child, and every case of hysteria must begin in childhood, when a person is most helpless.

If Freud expected the world to eagerly take up his discovery, he was mistaken. But he was right to recognize that he had created a new science, psychoanalysis. It was a science of the mind—in particular, a way to examine that part of the mind of which we are not aware, yet which influences every aspect of life: the unconscious mind.

7

A Loving Father and a Loving Son

Sigmund and Martha had six children. The babies made Freud happy. He named them after people he admired, just as he had named his brother Alexander. His oldest son, Jean Martin, was named after Dr. Charcot. That Freud was still ready to do battle, at least in his world of ideas, was shown by the choice of a name for his second son. He named him Oliver, after Oliver Cromwell, an English leader who opposed a powerful king and never lost a battle! Ernst was named after the beloved Professor Brücke. Mathilde, the name of Josef Breuer's wife, was chosen for Freud's oldest daughter. Sophie and Anna were named after relatives Sigmund and Martha loved and respected.

Their home was now at 19 Berggasse, in Vienna, where Freud also had his consulting rooms. He could come in to see his family and enjoy lunch with them or have a talk between patients' appointments. He and Martha were to live at this address for forty-seven years.

When Mathilde was a child of five, she became ill with diphtheria. There was no treatment for this disease, and the family feared she might die. Feverish, she called out for strawberries.

"How can I find strawberries, at this time of year?" Freud sighed, as he trudged out into the cold, windy street.

But he did return with them and brought them to her bedside. She took one in her mouth and tried to swallow. Instead, she coughed terribly.

"Ach, Martha, I fear for her," moaned Freud. But the coughing fit dislodged a plug of mucus from her throat. By the next morning, she was on her way to good health! Had her life been saved by a strawberry? No, the family knew it had been saved by a devoted father.

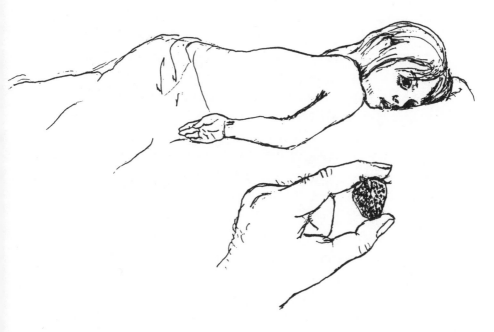

He brought the strawberries to her bedside.

Sigmund had always been a loving son. As far as he knew, he was grateful to his father for teaching him and caring for him through his life. He had helped to support his father when that became necessary. So when Jakob died, in 1896, Freud was struck by his reaction to his father's death. Why couldn't he go to the graveyard? Why did he now feel that his father had not liked him? Why did he have dreams that his father had kept him away from his beloved books?

One morning, soon after Jakob's death, Freud woke with a start. He had been dreaming. He dreamed that he was in a train station, traveling with an old gentleman who was blind. He, Freud, was disguised and wanted to stay that way. He had to help the old man urinate, as if he were his nurse.

The dream brought forth a memory. When he was a child, he had lost control and had urinated in his parents' room. His father had been angry and had said, "The boy will come to nothing."

This had wounded young Sigmund, and the wound had never healed. At least in the dream, he had restored good feelings about himself, the good feelings that he had lost when his father judged him so harshly. The blind old man in the dream must be his father, he reasoned. Sigmund had helped to restore his father's eyesight by assisting Carl Koller in an operation using cocaine. Now it was the old man, his father, who could not control his urinating. Sigmund is strong and powerful, a helper. He has avenged himself against his father, but he does not have to feel guilty. After all, is he not helping the old man?

If this interpretation was true, then dreams must have a purpose. They must satisfy wishes that the dreamer is afraid to recognize. When Freud was a child, he could not let himself think that he wanted to get even with his father. Otherwise, he might have lost control over his feelings and done something.

The big man, the father, would have really been angry with him and punished him. Better to forget it—well, at least to try to forget it.

In a dream, Freud thought, one can wish anything, because one cannot move or act on a wish that might be dangerous. Besides, dreams mix everything up so that the dreamer does not have to understand the dream in case he wishes for something forbidden. Freud wanted to understand his dreams.

He soon saw that understanding their own dreams could help his patients as it had helped him. He wrote about his own dreams, such as the one above, and other people's dreams in a most important book, *The Interpretation of Dreams*. It was published in 1900. Dreams, wrote Freud, are a part of normal life. They offer insight into people's feelings. Because the mind is unguarded during sleep, forbidden wishes can slip out. Even when they slip through, they are disguised. He showed how the mind disguises people and their actions to make them more acceptable to the dreamer, just as he had disguised his father and himself in the dream of the old man.

"Martha," he said one day, "my father's death was the most important thing that ever happened to me. It helped me understand myself. I now understand the anger, the hurt, and the love I felt toward my father."

8

Little Hans

Freud was going to Italy. He knew he loved travelling and had been lucky to go wherever he wished—Paris, Berlin, London—and now to Rome. But why was he still nervous and anxious, fearful to embark on trips? He now remembered his first journey, when he was taken away from his safe home on a frightening, roaring train. He understood now that he had been afraid of losing his parents, of being left alone. His keen mind took him from idea to idea.

Freud realized that every time he started to travel he felt the same fear, which he had forgotten long ago: the fear that he would lose his parents and their love. Here he was, an adult, still with the same fear! This fear did not serve him any longer. When he understood this, he felt easier about his trip.

Freud had described that patients also seemed to forget the very events that upset them. He said *seemed* to forget, because he believed that people did not really forget but pushed unpleasant

36

memories into a part of the mind that he called "the unconscious." Everyone has an unconscious mind where memories and wishes too frightening or painful to think about are stored.

In fact, Freud was able to show that all people may try to push some ideas or wishes out of their minds. Suddenly, the idea will pop out of hiding, show itself in a mistake, a "slip of the tongue." For instance, a man wrote to Freud, "I didn't know I was angry at my wife, until I said to her 'I want to kill—I mean, kiss you!' " Freud enjoyed collecting examples of slips of the tongue and published them in 1901 in a book which showed that many kinds of forgetting and errors of everyday life revealed unconscious intentions.

Many writings confirming his ideas followed. He had become interested in how the mind of the child works and in the ideas children have about the differences between the sexes and about childbirth. He saw how these unconscious ideas persisted in adult hysteria. In 1909, he published a case that was unusual even for him in those days. It was about the treatment of a five-year-old boy. Moreover, the treatment was carried out by the boy's father under Freud's supervision.

The father told Freud that his son would not leave the house because he was afraid a horse might bite him. Horses, wagons, and carriages were the major means of transportation in those times. It would have been almost impossible for the little boy to avoid a horse in the streets.

Over a period of time, Freud and the boy's father pieced together facts about the boy's fears. It turned out that the boy also seemed afraid of his father. Why would a son be afraid of a father as kind and loving as this one? Freud learned that after the birth of his sister, this young boy had felt excluded from his parents. He felt small in comparison to his father and displaced from his mother. He wanted his mother all to himself, but feared that his father would be angry with him and punish him. It was hard to live with these ideas, so the little boy pushed them out of his mind. Horses were big and strong, and so was his father. The boy must have connected horses with his father. It was easier to be afraid of horses than to be afraid of his father. One did not have to live with them or want their love. One could stay away from them by not going out on the street.

The father, with Freud's direction, helped his son understand the distortion of his ideas by talking to him and by bringing out his feelings. The boy understood that he would grow up and have a wife and child of his own. His fear of horses disappeared.

The boy was
afraid a horse
might bite him.

This case confirmed for Freud what he had learned from the treatment of adult patients—the disturbances of adult life begin in childhood. Here was a little boy who showed the same unexplainable fears that brought adults to treatment, and the little boy helped to explain what the fears meant.

Freud wrote about this case in detail, calling the boy "Little Hans." He also described several other cases in great detail, but they were of adults. With this case of Little Hans, he opened the door to the treatment of children's emotional problems through understanding.

Years later, it pleased Freud a great deal when a healthy young man knocked on his door at 19 Berggasse and introduced himself with the words, "I am Little Hans."

9

Friends

For years Freud had worked alone. He was the only doctor who practiced psychoanalysis. But gradually, a small group in Vienna began to use this treatment. One man, a doctor who had himself been helped by Freud's method, suggested that a group get together to discuss their work. Soon a small band of Viennese followers began to meet every Wednesday evening in Freud's offices. They called themselves the "Psychological Wednesday Society."

In 1906 a letter arrived from the director of a highly regarded hospital in Switzerland. The letter said that the hospital's doctors, led by Carl G. Jung, were applying the ideas of psychoanalysis to very sick patients. Freud was delighted by this news that his work had been recognized in another country. Letters between Jung and Freud began to fly back and forth.

One cold February morning the following year a tall man in fur cap and overcoat knocked on the apartment door of 19 Berggasse.

"Come in, come in, Herr Doctor Jung," Martha Freud welcomed the stranger. "My husband awaits you in the study. Good hot coffee with whipped cream awaits you too!"

Martha ushered in this gentleman with pleasure, for she knew of Doctor Jung. She anticipated that the two men would talk for hours, for her husband had looked forward to discussions with this man who had traveled to Vienna for this purpose. And, indeed, Freud was so excited by Jung's intelligence and lively imagination that he listened to Jung talk, without interruption, for three solid hours! Then, it was Freud's turn.

Freud's ideas about the mind came mostly from his work with his own patients. These people came into his office voluntarily because they were suffering. They realized that something was wrong with them. They were somewhat confused about what was real and what was imaginary, and that confusion bothered them. In general, they knew very well the difference between what was real and what was imaginary. They certainly could tell the difference between a dream and real life. They were able to live outside of hospitals in their homes; usually, they were able to work. They could cooperate with the doctor in the treatment. The illnesses of these patients were generally called "neuroses."

Jung, on the other hand, worked in a mental hospital. Many of the patients there were sicker than the neurotic patients who came to Freud's office. Usually, they did not come to a hospital on their own. Unlike the neurotics, they could not tell the difference between what was real and what was imaginary. They might have bizarre beliefs, and their judgment was so poor that they could not take care of themselves. They might believe that someone else was causing their problems or was trying to harm them. They seemed as if they were sick beyond suffering, so sick that they did not feel that they were sick at all or that anyone could help or treat them. Such patients were called "psychotics." Jung found that Freud's ideas about hysteria could help him in the treatment of these patients also.

Freud was excited that psychoanalysis could help Jung and his colleagues understand the minds of psychotic patients. He knew that psychoanalysis could explain something about every human mind—the well, the neurotic, and the psychotic. They parted that day as good friends.

Carl Jung visited Freud at 19 Berggasse.

In 1908, Jung organized an international meeting for the presentation of "Freudian psychology." People came from England, Hungary, Germany, Switzerland, and even distant America to read and hear papers on psychoanalysis. Freud was gratified by this meeting, held in Salzburg, Austria. It was to be only the first of many such international meetings. They were important not only because they acclaimed Freud's ideas but because they tested and expanded them.

At the end of that year, Freud, looking over his mail, saw the stamps of a foreign country on one envelope. When he had torn it open, he saw that he was invited to come to Clark University in Massachusetts to give a series of lectures on psychological subjects and also to receive the honorary degree of Doctor of Laws. The letter was signed by Stanley Hall, President of Clark University.

"Marty," Sigmund called up the stairs, "I am going to Niagara Falls!"

Freud was joking. He was reducing the meaning of this trip to America to mere sightseeing. But he was honored to be offered the degree of Doctor of Laws and to be invited to speak as an authority on psychoanalysis.

When he learned that Carl Jung too was invited, he felt that the invitation was even more significant. Freud asked his good friend Sandor Ferenczi to accompany him, and the three men booked passage on the ship *George Washington* in the summer of 1909.

The day before he and his friends were to leave, Freud gave a luncheon. After convincing Jung to drink wine, a practice to which Jung had been opposed, Freud fell down in a faint! When he recovered, ideas swirled about in his mind. Why had he fainted? Was it the food he had been eating? Was it lack of sleep? Was he anxious about the trip? Perhaps, but he felt there was another answer. Jung was his respected colleague. Was Freud angry with him? Was he envious of him? Freud puzzled over his feelings, wanting to understand, in the same way that he wanted to understand the meanings of dreams.

A few years later, once more after being able to convince Jung about an issue, he again fainted. He came to see the similarity between his rivalrous relationship to Jung and that of one to a baby brother who had died. As a child he had interpreted the death as resulting from the magical power of his wishes. Now, unconsciously to protect Jung from the same fate, he fainted.

He wrote Martha from the ship about the weather, about his dreams, and about fainting. The crossing was pleasant. One afternoon, Freud came across his cabin steward leaning against the ship's railing, reading. Freud noticed with pleasure and surprise that the man was reading Freud's book about slips of the tongue and about the unconscious in everyday life. The steward looked up when he saw Freud. "This all rings true," said the young man. "I recognize myself in it many times over."

"Now," mused Freud, "I have the notion that I might be famous."

They docked at New York City and were soon swept up in the excitement and bustle of energetic America. Chinatown, Columbia University, beautiful green Central Park, and the Metropolitan Museum of Art amazed and amused the Europeans. Coney Island Park, with its large Ferris wheel, reminded them of Vienna's Prater Park. American food made their stomachs ache, and the first moving picture they had ever seen, a mad chase, made their eyes blink.

They sailed to New York City.

When they arrived at Clark University, Freud found that a friendly and distinguished audience of doctors, university professors, and scholars were assembling to hear his talks.

"I have nothing written down," he told Ferenczi nervously. "Come walk with me, and help me decide what I will tell my American audience."

Freud delivered five lectures that week, in flowing, conversational German, about the history of psychoanalysis and his cases and about dreams and their meanings. He left Massachusetts feeling that psychoanalysis was, if not accepted, at least well known enough to be controversial in the New World.

At last, Freud journeyed to upstate New York to view Niagara Falls! No sight in Europe conveyed the same sense of power as Niagara's rushing water. As the boat approached the

Cave of the Winds, Freud heard the guide say over the roaring water, "Let the old fellow go first." He was only fifty-three years old, and this wounded his pride. His delight turned to dismay. Was he already growing old?

When Freud returned to Vienna, he called America "a gigantic mistake." Even his friends did not know why. His trip was lively, but he said the food upset his stomach! His ideas were received well enough, but when he spoke English, he was hurt to discover that he could not be clearly understood.

Although this trip to America made Sigmund Freud renowned, back home in Vienna the medical world continued to ignore him. The Vienna Medical Society withheld membership from him. And, although the International Psychoanalytical Association was formed in 1910, some of his closest friends and colleagues, including Carl Jung, later defected from the group.

10

Enemies All Around

In the summer of 1915, Freud and his companions were sitting in a coffeehouse in the rocky hills not far from Vienna. The air was clear, and one could look for miles over the peaceful landscape. Other than the watery coffee and the outrageously expensive whipped cream, there was no sign that this quiet land was engaged in a bloody world war.

The men exchanged jokes that were circulating in Vienna about the shortages of food and supplies and about the high prices, but Freud was grim. He was worried about his sons at the front.

Ferenczi said, "Adler says the war proves him right, that Kaiser Wilhelm started the war to overcome his humiliation about his withered arm." Alfred Adler, a Viennese psychoanalyst, had been an early follower of Freud but now disagreed with him about the importance of love in mental illness. People, said Adler, behaved irrationally not for want of love but to

From the coffee house, one could look for miles
over the peaceful landscape.

overcome the sense of their own inferiority, especially if there
was some defect in their bodies, like the Kaiser of Germany,
who had a crippled arm. A lively discussion began on the subject,
but Freud interrupted.

Freud explained that Kaiser Wilhelm reacted, not because
he was humiliated by his arm, but because his mother had been
unable to love him because of it.

There seemed no more to be said about it. The group became
quieter, wondering if the illness of one leader could plunge a
whole world into destruction.

Freud's mind leaped ahead as he tried to understand why
people followed a leader. He looked again toward the notion of
love. It must also be that followers seek the leader's love, the
way children seek the love of their parents.

On the train back to Vienna, he thought, "I must study this
question further. The ways of love are often unexpected."

Rumor came, in 1918, that Jean Martin's platoon had been taken prisoner on the Italian front. The family had no word of him for many weeks. Sigmund and Martha had great anxiety, for they knew how terrible the conditions could be in a prisoner-of-war camp. Prisoners often died of infections. Soon a card arrived that said Jean Martin was in an Italian hospital. He remained there for many months.

When the war ended, all three sons miraculously returned safely, and the Freud family was reunited. The war years had taken a terrible toll. Gradually, however, Sigmund and Martha were able to enjoy, in peace and leisure, the marriages of their children and the births of grandchildren. By 1920, five of Freud's children were married, and he delighted in this large and healthy family.

What a sad irony that, having survived the war without death, Freud's beautiful and beloved daughter Sophie died suddenly of pneumonia early in 1920. More grief came to the Freuds when Sophie's little son Heinz, called Heinerle, a most beloved grandchild, died three years later. He told a friend that this loss had killed something inside him for good. Then in the same year, 1923, doctors discovered that he had cancer of the jaw.

The cancer in his jaw and the many operations that followed caused him great pain. Years before, he had written a paper in which he compared a patient with a mental illness to a person with a toothache. The person, in either case, cannot care very much about anyone else because all of his interest is in himself, in his own pain and on how to relieve it. Now Freud had the pain in his own jaw. But he was able to retain his interest in the world around him. In discomfort himself, he turned his attention to the cruel and destructive side of human beings and began to write about how people live with each other in society despite their conflicts and difficulties.

11

The Final Years

Freud had explored the idea of how and why people look for a leader to rule them, and he had published his insights in a book about the psychology of groups. The desire for a strong leader may cause a people, in a sense, to fall in love with someone who seems strong and, by feeling at one with him, to feel strong themselves. The leader may take the people into war and ruin. Freud now feared what was happening in Germany. He saw the German people adoring a leader named Adolf Hitler.

Freud feared that humanity would plunge itself into another bloody war, like World War I, and he signed and circulated an appeal to the Geneva Anti-War Congress in 1932. He urged that doctors of all countries, knowing firsthand the horrors of war, try to stop another world war from starting. He asked them to "raise [their] . . . voices in warning against a new international bloodbath." His words were in vain, however, for in that year the Nazis came to power in Germany. In the first month of 1933,

Adolf Hitler became chancellor of Germany. The "international bloodbath" had begun.

Freud heard with dismay that his books, along with the writings of other great thinkers, had been publicly burned. He commented, "What progress we are making. In the Middle Ages they would have burnt me; nowadays they are content with burning my books."

The Nazis publicly burned the books.

In 1938, German tanks roared through the city of Vienna. Soldiers swarmed through the streets. Great crowds of people shouted, "Heil Hitler!" Soldiers invaded the houses and shops of Jews, and soon many Jews were taken away to concentration camps.

One day there was a loud knocking at 19 Berggasse. Nazi police forced their way into the Freud apartment. They demanded money. Martha put the money they had at home on the table and asked them to "help themselves," as if she were a gracious hostess serving dinner. Anna was forced to open the safe in the next room, which they emptied. The following day Anna was taken away and questioned by the Nazis. Although she was released that night, shock and fear numbed the Freuds.

Now the many famous and influential friends that Freud had made in his lifetime begged him to leave Vienna. But that was not easy for Freud. At first, he refused to think of giving up his home of almost eighty years. His sisters and their families lived there. He was sick and weak, and travelling would be difficult. Even if he could manage the trip, would the Nazis allow them to leave? His caring friends urged Freud to push these hesitations aside. They worked hard to get permits for the Freuds to leave, and they succeeded.

On June 5, 1938, Sigmund, Martha, and Anna boarded a train for England. Reunion with the rest of his children followed. Freud's final journey must have been sadder and more frightening than his first train ride. The danger in which he left his sisters and their families, who were unable to get permits, was real and terrible. He could not foresee that his sisters were to die in concentration camps when he later wrote to a friend, " . . . in spite of everything I still greatly loved the prison [Austria] from which I have been released."

A great welcome awaited him in London. Newspaper head-
lines proclaimed the arrival of Professor Freud. Flowers filled
the house where the family went to live. He felt at home in
England; all his life, since his trip when he was nineteen, he had
wanted to live and work there. No doubt his ideas would have
found easier acceptance there than in Austria.

For one year and three months, the Freuds lived in material
comfort. However, Freud felt unbearable pain from his can-
cerous jaw. On September 23, 1939, he requested morphine from
his doctor to help ease his unbearable pain, in an amount large
enough to put him to a peaceful death. He died, at eighty-three
years of age.

12

Freud's Legacy

Sigmund Freud was a bold and courageous man, an explorer of the mind who discovered psychoanalysis. This "talking treatment" opened up a kind of window into the unconscious minds of his patients. Memories of hurts and defeats that were too painful to recall could be experienced in the present, relived, and understood with the help of a doctor. The patient could be helped to understand the difference between the present and the past, to see both realistically, and to be freer for work and love.

We are all influenced by fears and wishes of our childhood that are unknown to us. Freud changed the way all people think about themselves, not only those who are patients. At first, only a small group of educated people could see that the unconscious mind has an effect on how one behaves. Today there is hardly a person, educated or not, who does not believe that the unconscious mind exerts a force on our lives.

One result of this view was to influence how people treat children. Freud enlarged people's view of how children think and feel. All events in a child's life, including nursing and weaning, the toilet training of a toddler, growing toward and away from the parents, sexual experience and education, how a child is made to feel about the body, and the care of the sick child, had meaning. How a child dealt with these events would influence the outcome of the rest of his life. Tantrums, jealousies, bad dreams, and strange fears were not signs of an evil nature that had to be crushed. Instead, the reasons for them could be understood to help the child. Children differed in their emotional needs, and their needs changed at different stages of their lives. Freud showed us that love, nurturing, and strong family relationships are of utmost importance for the growing child.

Freud left a legacy of ideas and words that have become part of our everyday knowledge and language. It is common to talk about feeling guilty or hostile, of being aggressive, of making a slip of the tongue. Freud has shown the importance of trying to understand why we can't remember certain occurrences and of paying attention to our dreams.

Another legacy of Freudian thought is that many people want to be more honest about their feelings and more honest in relationships with other people. We are not responsible for our feelings, Freud showed us. We are responsible, instead, for our behavior. Freud thought that people should accept all their thoughts and feelings, not all their actions. Children who had "bad" thoughts or unpleasant dreams once might have been punished for them; Freud helped us see that how we act is more important in showing our real character. We can think and feel whatever we want to! In fact, the best hope for us to act reasonably is to be aware of our thoughts and feelings, even when they seem most unreasonable.

It is hard to imagine a world without the influence of Sigmund Freud. When we look at an artist's work, think about how a writer tells a story, hear a fairy tale or myth, or ponder why there is war instead of peace, we know that unconscious thoughts and feelings influence all that humans do and create. There is unconscious meaning in every human act, even if we cannot always know what the meaning is.

Freud has been dead for more than forty-five years. He left behind twenty-three volumes of published works. Today there are thousands of psychoanalysts who practice psychoanalysis much as Freud developed it. But many thousands more, both doctors and other therapists, use "talking treatments" based on some of the ideas of psychoanalysis. Scientists eagerly continue to study the mind, adding to and challenging Freud's contributions. Freud would have been interested in these challenges, for above all, Freud was a seeker of the truth.

In a letter celebrating his eightieth birthday, 191 of the most esteemed writers and artists of the twentieth century signed a congratulatory address that said: " . . . this courageous seer and healer has for two generations been a guide to hitherto undreamed-of regions of the human soul . . . . a thinker and investigator who knew how to stand alone . . . he went his way and penetrated to truths which seemed dangerous because they revealed what had been anxiously hidden, and illumined dark places . . . . never again will the questions be stilled which Sigmund Freud put to mankind . . . his achievement has left a deep mark; and, we feel sure, if any deed of our race remains unforgotten it will be his deed of penetrating into the depths of the human mind."

Important Dates in Sigmund Freud's Life

May 6, 1856	Born in Freiberg, Moravia
1859	Moves to Leipzig, Germany
1860	Moves to Vienna, Austria
1865	Enters Sperlgymnasium
1873-1881	Studies medicine at University of Vienna
1875	First journey to England
1877	Publishes first article, on nerve cells of primitive fish
1879-1880	Serves in Austrian army
March 31, 1881	Graduates from medical school
1882	Meets and becomes engaged to Martha Bernays
1882-1885	Trains at Vienna General Hospital
1884-1887	Studies uses and effects of cocaine
1885-1886	Studies in Paris with neurologist Charcot
April 1886	Opens private practice in Vienna
September 1886	Marries Martha Bernays in Wandsbek, Germany
October 1886	Reads paper on hysteria to Vienna Medical Society
1891	Moves to and opens office at 19 Berggasse
1896	First uses the term *psychoanalysis*
1900	*The Interpretation of Dreams* is published
1904	*The Psychopathology of Everyday Life* is published
1907	Meets Carl Jung
1908	Vienna Psycho-Analytical Society is formed (formerly Psychological Wednesday Society)
1908	First International Psychoanalytical Congress is held in Salzburg, Austria
1909	Travels to Clark University, Massachusetts
1910	International Psychoanalytical Association is formed
1914-1918	World War I
1920	Daughter Sophie dies at age twenty-six
1923	Grandson Heinz dies at age four
1923	Cancer is discovered in his jaw
March 1938	Nazis take over Austria
June 1938	Freuds leave Vienna for London
September 23, 1939	Dies at age eighty-three

Further Reading

Berger, Gilda. *Mental Illness*. New York: Franklin Watts, Inc., 1981.

Freud, Ernst, Freud, Luci, and Grubrich-Simitis, Ilse, eds. *Sigmund Freud: His Life in Pictures and Words*. With a biographical sketch by K.R. Eissler. New York: Harcourt Brace Jovanovich, 1978.

Hirsch, S. Carl. *Theater of the Night What We Do and Do Not Know About Dreams*. Chicago: Rand McNally & Co., 1976.

Hyde, Margaret O. *Is the Cat Dreaming Your Dream*. New York: McGraw-Hill Book Co., 1980.

Kettelkamp, Larry. *Hypnosis: The Wakeful Sleep*. New York: William Morrow & Co., Inc., 1975.

    Your Marvelous Mind. Philadelphia: Westminster Press, 1980.

Klagsbrun, Francine. *Sigmund Freud*. New York: Franklin Watts, Inc., 1967.

LeShan, Eda. *What Makes Me Feel This Way: Growing up with Human Emotions*. New York: Macmillan Publishing Co., Inc., 1974.

Litowinsky, Olga and Willoughby, Bebe. *The Dream Book*. New York: Coward, McCann and Geoghegan, Inc., 1978.

Neimark, Anne E. *Sigmund Freud: The World Within*. New York: Harcourt Brace Jovanovich, Inc., 1976.

Poole, Lynne and Gray. *Scientists Who Changed the World*. New York: Dodd, Mead & Co., 1962.

Wilson, John Rowan and the Editors of Time-Life Books. *The Mind*. Alexandria, Virginia: Time-Life Books, revised edition, 1980.

Index